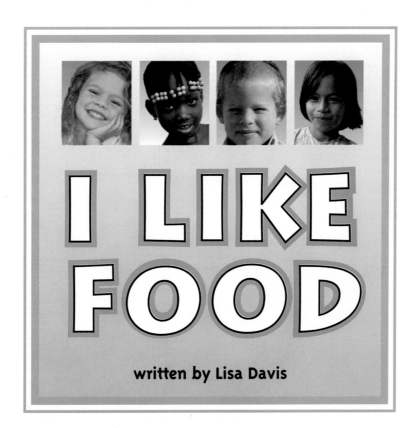

I LIKE FOOD

written by Lisa Davis

Harcourt

Orlando Boston Dallas Chicago San Diego

Visit *The Learning Site!*

www.harcourtschool.com

I like pizza.

I like rice.

I like soup.

I like bread.

I like fish.

I like pancakes.

Israel

United States
of America

Ghana

Russia

Ethiopia

Philippines

Acknowledgements:
Cover: Background (tl) FoodPix; (tr) George Mattei/Envision ; (cl) Paul Webster/Tony Stone Images; (cr) Paul A. Souders/Corbis; (bl) Steven Needham/Envision; (br) FoodPix; Center Inset (l) Dennie Cody/FPG International; (cl) Bob Burch/Bruce Coleman, Inc.; (cr) Paul A. Souders/Corbis; (r) Tony Arruza/Bruce Coleman, Inc.
Page 2 Chris Everard/Tony Stone Images; 3 (l) Dennie Cody/FPG International; 3 (cl) Bob Burch/Bruce Coleman, Inc.; 3 (cr) Paul A. Souders/Corbis; 3 (r) Tony Arruza/Bruce Coleman, Inc.; 4 Chris Everaed/Tony Stone Images; 4 (bg) FoodPix; 5 Dennie Cody/FPG International; 6 Ken Kinzie/Harcourt; 6 (bg) Paul Webster/Tony Stone Images; 7 Bob Burch/Bruce Coleman, Inc.; 8 (c), (bg) Steven Needham/Envision; 9 Michele Burgess/The Stock Market; 10 FoodPix; 10 (bg) George Mattei/Envision; 11 Paul A. Souders/Corbis; 12 Paul A. Souders/Corbis; 12 (bg) PhotoDisc; 13 Tony Arruza/Bruce Coleman, Inc.; 14 Penny Cash/FoodPix; 14 (bg) FoodPix; 15 Robin Smith/FPG International; 16-17 (bg) Worldsat International and J. Knighton/Photo Researchers; 16 (li) Dennie Cody/FPG International; 16 (tri) Paul A. Souders/Corbis; 16 (bri) Bob Burch/Bruce Coleman, Inc.; 17 (li) 9 Michele Burgess/The Stock Market; 17 (tri) Robin Smith/FPG International; 17 (bri) Tony Arruza/Bruce Coleman, Inc.; 18 (bg) Paul Webster/Tony Stone Images; 18 Ken Kinzie/Harcourt.